How to Start a YouTube Channel for Fun & Profit!

By
Ann Eckhart

Table of Contents

INTRODUCTION 1

CHAPTER 1: CREATING YOUR YOUTUBE &
ADSENSE ACCOUNTS.. 7

CHAPTER 2: FILMING EQUIPMENT & SET-UP 13

CHAPTER 3: YOUR CHANNEL'S THEME & CONTENT...............20

CHAPTER 4: HOW TO EARN MONEY ON YOUTUBE.................29

CHAPTER 5: MARKETING 35

CHAPTER 6: BEST PRACTICES...59

CHAPTER 7: DAY IN THE LIFE...72

CONCLUSION..82

ABOUT THE AUTHOR..84

INTRODUCTION

In 2005, I started a home-based gift basket business, which soon transitioned into an online gift shop selling ceramics, books and plush. For years, I sold new gift items successfully on both Ebay and Amazon. Unfortunately, as more retailers, and even my wholesalers, started selling online directly to customers, I found myself squeezed out of the gift trade.

Fortunately, I had done some "picking" here and there, so I had vintage and secondhand items to fall back on as a source of goods to resell. However, I definitely needed to educate myself more on what items to look for to sell on Ebay; and that is how I found YouTube!

I initially turned to YouTube in search of videos from people who, like me, sold on Ebay. I quickly discovered a YouTube "picking community" (now called the "reseller community") full of people who bought items at garage sales and thrift stores to resell on Ebay. These fellow resellers offered me a huge wealth of information as I transitioned out of selling new gift items and began focusing solely on secondhand treasures.

I began interacting with a small group of YouTubers, commenting on their videos and offering what advice I could to help them with selling on Ebay. After a few months, I finally got the courage to jump in with my own videos, showing items I picked up at estate sales to resell on Ebay. I shot the videos on my iPhone, and I was able to easily upload them to YouTube. The more videos I shared, the more subscribers I got. I was having a lot of fun making videos and interacting with fellow

Ebayers, so I didn't even notice that I was missing out on another benefit of YouTube: making money!

I started my first YouTube channel without even considering the possibility that it could make me money. Because I didn't do my research beforehand, I didn't know that I hadn't set up my channel to properly connect with AdSense, which is the Google advertising platform for YouTube. So, while I continued to make videos and gain subscribers, I wasn't earning a penny.

It wasn't until I started my blog, first called SeeAnnSave but now at AnnEckhart.com, that I figured out my mistake. While setting up my blog and going through the AdSense process to monetize it, I got a notice that I could also create a YouTube channel, connect it with my new AdSense account, and earn money from both my blog AND my videos.

What a second, I thought; but I already have a YouTube channel! Why can't THAT channel earn me money? Turns out I hadn't signed up with Google for my first channel, so it was unable to earn AdSense money. The new channel that Google offered me when I signed up for AdSense on my blog, however, WAS through Google. And therefore, my new channel could be monetized and make me money.

Confused? So was I! I now had TWO YouTube channels, one with all of my content and subscribers that wasn't earning me anything; and a new channel that had no subscribers but had the potential to bring in some cash.

For a while, I tried keeping both channels active. However, I quickly ditched the channel that wasn't making me any money and focused on the one that was. I eventually ended up deactivating that first channel altogether, so it isn't even on You Tube's site now.

After I made the decision to delete the videos on my old channel, I began the process of trying to direct those subscribers to my new channel. Initially some subscribers were upset that my old videos were gone, but it ended up working out as I reshot those videos and was able to provide better quality and content on my new channel.

In order to encourage people to subscribe to my new YouTube channel, I did giveaways, handing out $10 Amazon gift cards every time I reached a new subscriber goal (250, 500, 750, 1000). Before long, my new channel had far more subscribers than my old channel ever had, I was producing better content, AND I was making money!

A few years back I started a second (or I guess it's technically my third) YouTube channel devoted to Walt Disney World vacation vlogs. However, I ended up moving those videos to my main channel and for a couple of years that second channel sat stagnant.

In 2019, I started expanding the content that was on my main YouTube channel to include lifestyle videos such as shopping hauls and unboxings. I realized that I while I loved that sort of content, having both reselling AND lifestyle videos on the same channel wasn't working. Since my reselling videos bring in the most AdSense, I made the decision to start posting daily reselling vlogs on my second channel, remaining it SeeAnnSell. I then dedicated my main channel, Ann Eckhart, to lifestyle content.

Why did I move the videos that bring in the most AdSense to the smaller channel? Because on YouTube you are paid by VIEWS, not subscribers. I get the same number of views on my Ebay videos regardless of which channel they are on. However, while I do make AdSense money on the lifestyle videos posted on my first channel, I actually make more money by getting free products and sponsorships. On YouTube, it's not only AdSense that brings in the cash, but also sponsorships. Don't worry; I'll discuss all of the ways to make money on YouTube in-depth in this book!

Today, I devote my main channel to lifestyle content such as shopping hauls and product reviews while keeping my Ebay related videos on my second channel. So, as of this writing, I'm posting up to 14 videos a week to two different YouTube channels. Yes, I realize this sounds crazy! But I love making YouTube videos – and earning AdSense – and dividing my content between two channels allows me to upload more and make more money!

In this book, I am going to share with you how to easily and effectively start a YouTube channel for both fun AND profit. The fun part should always be your first priority when making videos. If you are going to put yourself out there in front of potentially millions of strangers, you want to make sure you are doing it because you WANT to, not because you think it will make you rich.

The fact of the matter is, while there are some very wealthy YouTubers out there, the vast majority of people making videos are simply earning a bit of extra money. Unless you get hundreds of thousands of subscribers and tens of thousands on views on your videos, you are likely looking at simply earning some extra money, perhaps building it up to part-time income status, through AdSense.

Making YouTube videos has helped me build my brand as it drives traffic to my blog, books, and social media accounts. I make money on YouTube not only from AdSense but also from sponsorships. And I get a lot of free products sent to me by companies. By consistently working on growing my channel, I now not only have a lot of FUN creating content, but I am also earning MONEY!

So, if you are ready to dive in to creating a YouTube channel of your own for fun and profit, let's get started!

CHAPTER 1

CREATING YOUR YOUTUBE & ADSENSE ACCOUNTS

Take the time to properly set up your YouTube and AdSense accounts before you start filming so that when your videos do go live, you can focus on the fun AND the profits!

Since Google owns YouTube and controls the AdSense advertising that pays you for your videos, you must first sign up with Google in order to start a channel. When I started my first YouTube channel, I didn't sign up through Google but instead registered through a different email account. Because I didn't sign up through Google, my first channel never earned me any money. You MUST register with Google in order to earn money from your YouTube channel!

Google Account: To sign up for Google and to create a YouTube account, head to accounts.google.com. The sign-up process is completely FREE; you create a Google account, a YouTube account, a Google email, and a YouTube channel, all in one place. Simply follow the online prompts to complete the process.

Channel Name: Choose your YouTube channel name with care. Google usually prompts you to make it your actual name, but you can choose anything you like (as long as it isn't currently being used). While you may just be starting out on YouTube for fun now, you don't want to limit yourself from growing your "brand" in the future. There are a lot of established, successful YouTube channels out there with names unrelated to their content because the people behind them never anticipated how large their channels would grow.

My first YouTube channel was my Ebay store name, the name that my reselling business was registered under. When I started my blog, I originally called it "SeeAnnSave"; I then worked to "brand" that name across all of my social networking sites, including starting a second (and what is now my main) YouTube channel. However, in late 2017 I rebranded to just my name, "Ann Eckhart". I had to rename not only my YouTube channel but all of my social media accounts. It was a huge undertaking; so, think long and hard before naming your channel to avoid the headache of changing it later on.

Note that your channel name is the same name on your Google account; changing your Google name will automatically change your YouTube channel name. However, the URL of your channel can only be changed by contacting YouTube directly. My main channel URL still ends with "seeannsave"; and my second channel URL ends with "seeannatwdw" as I initially started it as a Walt Disney World vlog channel. Now my main channel NAME is "Ann Eckhart" and my second channel NAME is "SeeAnnSell", even though the URL's haven't changed. It's confusing, I know!

AdSense Account: While you used to be able to start earning money right out of the gate on YouTube, in 2019 Google changed the requirements for becoming monetized. Now a channel needs to have 1,000 subscribers AND 4,000 hours of views before it can start earning AdSense money.

While these new requirements are frustrating for new YouTube creators, with dedication you can get your channel to monetization standards rather quickly. I'll go over ways to grow your channel later on in this book.

Once you've met Google's requirements for earning AdSense on your YouTube channel, you can apply to monetize it by signing up for an

AdSense account at GoogleAdSense.com. The AdSense application process is a little involved and will require you do go through several verification steps before you are approved to earn ad revenue. These days it's taking a couple of weeks to complete the process to start earning AdSense on YouTube. But once you do, all of your old videos, the ones you uploaded when you first started your channel, will also be able to earn money.

You can choose to have your AdSense earnings mailed to you or sent to you via direct deposit to your bank account. You must reach $100 in total AdSense earnings across all platforms in order to receive a payout. Since I have AdSense through both my blog and YouTube, I easily meet that $100 threshold every month; and the money is automatically deposited into my bank account towards the end of the month. At the end of the year, Google sends me a tax form detailing my earnings, which I give to my accountant so that he can add it to my income tax returns. Yes, you have to report your YouTube earnings to the IRS!

Monetize Your Videos: Your videos must be monetized in order for them to start earning income. Monetization means you are authorizing YouTube to place ads in your videos and that you are agreeing that no copyrighted materials (music and video clips from TV shows, movies or other copyrighted sources) appear in your footage.

Having an AdSense account doesn't automatically mean your videos will earn money; you need to manually monetize each of your videos. This is done in the YouTube Studio section of your YouTube account.

Simply click on a video and then click on the "Video Monetization" tab on the left-hand side of the page. Choose "On" from the Monetization drop-down menu. Then check every box under the "Type of ads" section. Click "Save" to finalize applying AdSense ads to that video. Make sure to go back into your old videos to monetize them, too.

I'll be going into more detail about how to upload, edit, and prepare your videos in for release in Chapter 7: Day in The Life.

YouTube Partnership: After you have created your Google, YouTube and AdSense accounts, there is one more step you will need to take before you can start earning money on your videos, and that is to become a YouTube Partner. Once your channel reaches 1,000 subscribers and 4,000 watch hours, YouTube will prompt you to sign up as partner.

Here is an abbreviated YouTube Partner Program application checklist:

- Make sure your channel follows all policies and guidelines as your channel will go through a review process. YouTube consistently monitors channels to ensure they are continually complying with their rules and regulations.

- Sign YouTube Partner Program terms by signing into YouTube, clicking on your profile picture, and choosing "YouTube Studio". In the left menu, click "Monetization". If you are under the 1,000 subs/4,000 hours threshold, click

"Notify me when I'm eligible" and you'll receive an email when you are able to apply. If you are ready to apply, sign the term and YouTube will mark it with a green "Done" sign on the "Review Partner Program Terms" card.

- Make sure you only have ONE AdSense account. You can link as many channels as you'd like to a single AdSense account. If you don't have an account, there will be on-screen prompts to help you create one.

- After your AdSense account is connected, YouTube will make it with a green "Done" sign.

- Wait for your channel to be reviewed. The review process currently takes less than a month; some people are approved within days while it takes others longer. It just depends how many channels are also in line for review. You'll be notified once the review is complete with instructions for monetizing your videos.

While the monetization process can seem overwhelming, don't be discouraged. Keep plugging away as you only have to do it one time; and it will all be worth it once you start earning money!

CHAPTER 2

FILMING EQUIPMENT & SET-UP

You don't need a professional studio full of high-tech equipment to create great YouTube videos. By following a few basic tips and tricks, you can produce high-quality videos right from your bedroom!

My guess is that you are anxious for this section because you want me to tell you exactly which camera you need to film your videos with and what computer you need to edit them on, right? Well, because there are so many different ways to upload videos, and new cameras and equipment are being released all of the time, you will need to do your research to find out how to upload and edit using the tools you have. Fortunately, there are a ton of YouTube videos out there to walk you through the uploading and editing process for your particular camera and computer.

However, as a basic guideline, you want a camera that can film in HD, whether 720p or 1080p. HD (high-definition) is the highest quality filming available for personal cameras and results in video footage that appears super crisp and clear. Most phones even film in HD these days, including the iPhone that I use. While I upload from my iPhone directly to YouTube, if you use a stand-alone camera, you will need to transfer your video footage to your computer via the camera's SD memory card.

Most YouTubers use Mac computers to edit their videos, using the iMovie software from Apple. I don't have a Mac computer, but since I film all of my videos on an Apple iPhone, I have access to the iMovie app, where I do all of my editing. You can also do some basic editing of your videos directly on YouTube. If you have a video camera on your computer, you can film directly on your computer onto YouTube's site.

If you have an iPhone, there is no reason you can't start filming your videos on that. It is certainly cheaper and easier than buying a camera and a Mac computer and then teaching yourself how to film and edit videos. However, as I said, there are so many ways you can film and upload that it is worth doing some research to see which options will work best for you. Internet searches of "what camera to use for filming YouTube videos" and "how to upload and edit YouTube videos" will yield hundreds of results. If you already have a camera, simply do a search for how to film and upload using your model to see what advice is available.

I have always filmed my videos on an iPhone; I have upgraded my iPhone four times since I started on YouTube, and each new phone offers better quality and faster processing. I simply use the camera feature to film my video, and then I put together the clips using the iMovie app. I then save the finished product to my camera roll, and from there I upload it to YouTube. After the video is uploaded, I then log on to YouTube from my computer (I have a PC, not a Mac), and finish the process from there. Easy!

No matter what you use to film on, quality is key. I film on my iPhone and upload the vast majority of my videos in High Definition (although sometimes my connection is glitchy and I have to upload in standard). I make sure I hold the camera steady and have plenty of light. I also hold the camera horizontally as filming vertically creates a black bar on either side of the video.

I have seen so many horrible YouTube videos where the footage is dark, the volume is on mute, and the screen is jerky. I have even seen videos that were upside down! Before you make your videos live, preview them first. While they don't have to be up to the Hollywood standard of film quality, you want them to be as clear and steady as possible. If a video looks bad to you when you are previewing it, imagine what viewers will think when you upload it.

Redo videos that aren't of good quality. Practice makes perfect! I have redone many videos during my time on YouTube. I would rather take the time to refilm a video than have a poor-quality clip be viewed by thousands of people.

There are few other things you can do to ensure your videos turn out great, no matter what camera, computer, or editing software you use:

Lighting: Full-time YouTubers often invest in professional lighting to make sure their footage is as crisp and clear as possible. However, you don't have to spend hundreds of dollars on lights and tripods, especially if you are just starting out.

I film in a room with lots of natural light and with the overhead lights on. While I do have a tripod, most of the time I don't even use it; I simply prop my iPhone up so that it is even with my face and film that way. If I find that the lighting in the room isn't sufficient, I simply turn on the auto light feature on my iPhone.

Speak Up: Another problem I see with a lot of YouTube videos from newbies is that the volume is so low that I can't even hear them speaking. When filming, make sure you are talking in a clear, loud voice. While you don't want to scream at viewers, you do want to make sure they can hear what you are saying. Make sure there is no background noise while you are filming, such as music or the television.

Backgrounds: You have likely seen YouTube videos with professionally designed backgrounds, as well as those shot in what looks to be the home of a hoarder. While you don't need to spend thousands of dollars to make the background of your videos look like it came straight from a home decor magazine, you also want to take care to film in a clean, clutter free space.

For sit-down videos, I have a dedicated space in my office where I film. I have bookshelves behind me; I change out the décor on the shelves seasonally. I will admit that, in the past, my backgrounds weren't as nice as I would have liked them to be, especially ones where there were piles of Ebay inventory behind me. I'm always trying to improve the quality of my videos, including my backgrounds.

One of my favorite backgrounds that I see a lot of female YouTubers use is to film with their bed behind them and twinkle lights (the kind you put on Christmas trees) strung up around the bed frame or window. This creates such a pretty scene for filming. Other people film with the nicest part of their kitchen or living room behind them. If you are serious about making YouTube your actual job, you will want to consider dedicating a space for filming that is well lit and nicely decorated. However, if you are just starting out or you are only interested in making a bit of money from YouTube, do the best with what you have. Some of the biggest YouTube channels on the site today got their start with the creators filming while sitting on the floor of their bedrooms!

Camera Angle: Finding the angle from which you look your best on camera can be a challenge. Most of us feel we have a "good side", the side of our face from which we look a bit more attractive than the other. However, video is much different from still photography in that you move around on film and aren't sitting in a stationery position. Therefore, it's more important to have the camera facing you directly as well as slightly above you. Having to look up a bit to the camera helps eliminate the double chin phenomenon!

As with background, camera angle is something I have always been challenged by. While I do have an iPhone tripod, it is a flimsy thing that doesn't hold my iPhone very well. I now have a handle on my phone that also converts to a stand; I can just prop the stand up on a flat surface to film. And the handle helps me hold the camera steady when I am vlogging.

Of course, if you choose not to appear on screen, you needn't focus on how you look but instead how on how what you are filming does, whether it is a single item or a moving scene. If you are filming cooking videos, for instance, you'll want a tripod that holds the camera to look over what you are preparing. Or perhaps you have someone else who can hold the camera and film you. Don't be surprised if your first videos don't look that great as it takes time to learn how to film best!

Keep It Classy: While you don't have to have your hair and make-up professionally done every time you film a YouTube video you do want to take care with your appearance. Looking as clean and neat as possible goes along way, even if you are just wearing jeans and a tee shirt. If you smoke, don't smoke on camera. And do your best to clean up your surrounding area. No one wants to see your overflowing trash can or pile of dirty laundry in the background of your videos.

CHAPTER 3

YOUR CHANNEL'S THEME & CONTENT

Millions of people use YouTube, making videos on everything from how to apply eye make-up to how to bake a cake. Finding a theme for your channel is important, although it's also okay to not limit yourself to one topic. Remember, keep it FUN and the profit will follow!

My first YouTube channel was dedicated solely to picking and reselling on Ebay. I didn't really talk about anything else on that channel; and the people who subscribed to me were there to learn and/or talk about Ebay. I didn't do videos to make money (and I didn't make any on my first channel); I simply enjoyed sharing my knowledge about reselling with others.

However, over the years I've experimented with different content on different channels; and for me personally, I've found it better to separate my lifestyle videos from my reselling videos and have them each on their own dedicated channels. Starting out, though, I would recommend just ONE channel. You definitely want to master running a single channel before you ever even think about have two or more. And most YouTube creators only have one channel. If I wasn't making videos about Ebay, I would only have one channel; reselling is such a small niche that it really does well with a dedicated channel.

I went into YouTube thinking that having a channel was like having your own television network. Unfortunately, that's not the way viewers see it. While you have NBC in your television channel line-up, it's likely that you only watch a few of their shows. However, you don't take NBC out of your TV package just because you don't watch every show they air.

YouTube, however, is different. YouTube itself is like a television network, and the individual channels are their own shows. You watch the shows, i.e. channels, you like. You don't watch ALL of the channels, but you still keep YouTube installed on your smart phone or tablet the way you have network stations on your TV.

Viewers subscribe and stay subscribed to channels because they like the "shows" (individual videos) they are seeing. If they don't like the "shows" you are producing, they may unsubscribe from your channel. The most loyal of my YouTube viewers watch the majority of videos I put out depending on which channel they are subscribed to. Some viewers watch all of the videos on both of my channels, while others only watch one channel. And still others only check in periodically depending on the video topic.

No matter what topic I am doing a video on or how much engagement I am getting between both of my channels, however, I try to only make videos that I WANT to make, ones that are FUN and INTERESTING to me. Even though I am now earning money on YouTube, the main reason I make videos is for my own personal enjoyment. YouTube has improved my public speaking skills and increased my confidence. It's allowed me to network and make new friends with people I would have never met otherwise. I make YouTube videos for FUN; and as a bonus, I also make money.

While I cover a wide variety of topics on my two YouTube channels, you may be looking to only do videos on one thing. Don't follow the trends in an effort to go with what is popular. Do videos about what you LOVE and the subscribers will follow.

Some common YouTube channel themes and video topics are:

Cooking & Baking: Do you love to cook and/or bake? If you are good in the kitchen, you can share your knowledge via YouTube videos. You don't have to be a master chef, either; even the simplest recipes are sought after on YouTube. I have several cooking and baking videos on my channel; all of my recipes are super easy to make but get quite a lot of views. Most are only a few minutes long, but they are some of my top-earning AdSense videos!

Crafting: Crafting is a huge category on YouTube, whether you want to do tutorials or simply show off your craft supply hauls and projects. Beading, scrapbooking, knitting, quilting, card making, and any other type of craft can make for great videos. The crafting community on YouTube is huge, so be sure to connect with other crafters who are making videos by liking and commenting on their videos, too. I'm not a crafter myself, but I have done well with some DIY Dollar Tree tutorials!

Diet & Fitness: Another hot YouTube channel theme is diet and fitness. Whether it is nutrition or weight loss, body building or running, lots of people turn to YouTube for help with getting in shape. Natural food and specialty diets (gluten-free, vegan, raw) are also popular video topics.

Gaming: Video game channels are among the most popular on YouTube. If you love to play video games, you can turn your hobby into income on YouTube.

Gardening: If you have a green thumb, consider sharing your gardening skills on YouTube. Lots of people want to learn about plants, flowers and vegetable gardening. Perhaps you can what you grow or sell it at a farmer's market. Share all of your gardening information and watch your subscriber list (and AdSense money) grow along with your plants!

Hauls: Love to shop? Share your shopping hauls with your YouTube subscribers. Even a trip to the grocery store to stock the fridge can make for an interesting video. I do quite a few haul videos on my personal YouTube channel from stores such as Dollar Tree, Bath & Body Works, and Target; and they are always a big hit.

How-To: As I talked about in the filming equipment section, there are thousands of how-to videos on nearly every topic, including how to film and edit YouTube videos. If there is an area or areas you are proficient in (computers, carpentry, crafting), creating how-to videos can be a great source of videos for your channel.

Make-up & Fashion: Beauty bloggers and vloggers are all over YouTube, and they are some of the most successful channels on the site. Most YouTube "beauty gurus" have an accompanying blog to support their videos and to earn more ad revenue. If you love make-up, skincare, and/or clothing, sharing your personal style tips with others may be the perfect theme for your channel.

In addition to doing make-up tutorials, beauty guru's also do first impression reviews of products, shopping hauls (from stores such as

ULTA, Sephora, and Bath & Body Works), make-up storage, make-up collections, nail polish collections, closet organization, jewelry collections, and clothing hauls. The beauty category is very crowded on YouTube. Only start a beauty channel because you LOVE make-up and clothes; if you are good at applying makeup and have a style that impresses others, the subscribers and ad revenue will follow.

Mommy Videos: Are you a mom-to-be or do you already have little ones in the home? There are lots of other moms out there you can connect with, whether it's simply sharing your baby's milestones or talking about what you feed your toddler. There are lots of women (and men!) out there who love to interact with other parents. Home schooling videos are also popular.

Organization: Organizing is another hot YouTube channel theme. How to organize your house, office, car, kid's toys, crafts, garage, and basement can all make for great videos. If you excel at organizing, you may think there isn't an audience for this topic, but believe me that there are people out there who would love to watch you organize something as simple as a junk drawer! Organizing your home on a budge from dollar stores is something a lot of people do videos on, too.

Picking/Reselling: I got started on YouTube by interacting with the "picking community" (now called "reselling community"), which is a group people who buy items from garage sales and thrift stores to resell on Ebay, Etsy, Poshmark, Amazon, or in antique mall booths. If you are a reseller, there are lots of people who would love to see your finds and hear about your sales. Sharing your tips about reselling both online and off will definitely gain you an audience.

Reviews: Do you love to read or go to the movies? Are friends always asking you to recommend your favorite video games or CD's? Do you always buy the latest gadgets? Millions of people turn to YouTube for reviews, so if you love books, movies, television, videos games, music, and/or electronics, consider making a channel where you offer your opinions! If you review products, you'll likely start to be contacted by companies offering to send you free items in exchange for video reviews. In just the past few months alone I've been sent a robotic vacuum, an air fryer, and a humidifier, all for free just for showing them on my YouTube channel.

If you do plan on doing reviews, note that copyright issues will prevent you from using clips of movies, video games, television shows, or music; but you can hold up your own copy of a DVD or CD if you want some sort of visual. Another way to make money on reviews is to sign up for an Amazon Associates account and put your referral link in the description bar to the item you are reviewing. If someone buys the item through your link, you will earn a commission. I'll talk more about this later on in this book.

Tags: Tags are very popular amongst YouTubers. Tags are simply question and answer lists, such as "50 Random Facts About Me". There are tags galore on YouTube, and they give you an easy way to create content as all you have to do is answer the questions. I even have a book entitled THE BIG BOOK OF YOUTUBE TAGS available that is filled with all sorts of tags you can film (the link to my Amazon Author Page is at the end of this book).

Travel: Do you love to travel? Perhaps you take frequent road trips or cruises or are an RV or camping enthusiast. There are lots of YouTube viewers who would love to see your travel footage, including your packing tips, dining recommendations, and money-saving advice. I've filmed many Walt Disney Vacation vlogs for my YouTube channel over the years.

Vlogging: People all over the world chronicle their lives through vlogs, many doing so every single day. I vlog every day on my SeeAnnSell reselling channel. It is very time consuming and can feel like an invasion of privacy if you aren't careful; however, lots of folks are earning a part-time and even full-time income on YouTube by sharing 10 to 20-minute snippets of their daily lives.

If you enjoy vlogging but don't want to commit to doing it every day, you can vlog whenever you are doing something particularly interesting or during a "vlogging month" such as "Vlogmas" (vlogging for Christmas), "Vlogtober" (vlogging every day in October), "VEDA" (vlogging every day in April), or "Vlogust" (vlogging every day in August). I, myself, have done "Vlogust" and "Vlogtober" in the past.

The hard part about vlogging for me has been that the subscribers who love the vlogs REALLY love the vlogs and desperately want them to continue on a daily basis. It's a lot of pressure to keep up with daily uploads. Another downside, for me at least, to vlogging is that you are exposing yourself to more criticism and scrutiny than a regular video might bring. Even when you only show 10-minutes out of a 24-hour day, viewers start to assume that they know everything about you and can be either overly friendly (i.e. a bit like a stalker!) or extremely critical.

Most daily vloggers start out interacting with viewers in the comments but stop doing that as their subscribers increase because they feel the need to more closely guard their privacy. If vlogging interests you, consider starting off by doing it once a week. You can always expand to more frequent vlogs if you decide you really enjoy doing them.

My Channels: As I talked about before, I first started my YouTube journey by sharing picking and reselling related videos. I did haul videos showing the items I bought at estate sales, Ebay and Amazon sales update videos, and Ebay tutorial videos. When I started my new channel, I at first only focused on lifestyle content, but eventually worked reselling into the mix. In between, I started and stopped a Disney World vlog channel. And today I've switched my content around again by uploading daily reselling vlogs to the former Disney channel and dedicating my personal channel to lifestyle content.

While maintaining two YouTube channels can be overwhelming, I have found that my videos are most successful (i.e. frequently viewed and commented on) when I do them first and foremost for myself. If I am having fun filming, viewers pick up on that and enjoy watching. As I have said several times already, have FUN and the profit will follow!

CHAPTER 4

HOW TO EARN MONEY ON YOUTUBE

AdSense isn't the only way to make money on YouTube! Referral and affiliate links, sponsorships, and selling your own products can also contribute to your overall YouTube earnings!

I've already discussed how you make money on YouTube via AdSense; but there are other ways you can bring in more income with your videos. While AdSense will be your first money-making stream, as you grow your channel, it likely won't be your last.

AdSense: I've already covered the basics of monetizing your videos with AdSense as a YouTube Partner. But it's important you understand how AdSense actually works, and how you can best utilize it on your channel.

AdSense is the route in which Google sells advertising. You have likely seen Google-branded pop-up ads on various websites; the money from those ads is processed through AdSense. When you are monetized on YouTube, Google will run ads on your videos; just like ads that appear on text-based websites, the ads that appear on videos are purchased and sold through AdSense. Google ads and AdSense are essentially one in the same.

Whether on a website or in a YouTube video, the ads that are displayed have been matched to the content. The ads are created and paid for by advertising companies. These companies pay Google to run the ads, and Google splits the money with the content creators.

On YouTube, how much money a video makes is determined by the CPM. CPM stands for "cost per 1,000 impressions". As a YouTube creator, you are paid per 1,000 views on all of your videos combined throughout the month. CPM's can be as low as $1 and as high as hundreds of dollars for large channels. The average CPM is $4 per 1,000 views, but it varies between every channel and can change daily.

Once you are monetized, you can track your CPM in the YouTube Studio area of your account. Simply click on the "Analytics" tab on the left side of the page to see your AdSense totals (you can customize the date range), and click on "Revenue" to see your CPM.

Affiliate Links: While AdSense is the main way most people earn money on YouTube, there is another way to bring in cash from your videos and that is through affiliate links. When you sign up with certain companies, you can get an affiliate link that will pay you a commission whenever someone buys an item through your link.

Amazon offers a popular referral program used by many YouTubers, including me. By signing up as an **Amazon Associate**, you can create referral links to any of the products on Amazon's website. Then if you use or mention a product in your video and provide a link to it in your YouTube video description box, you will earn a commission if anyone goes through your link to purchase that product. This is why you see many YouTube channels with Amazon product links in their description boxes.

In addition to Amazon, there are all kinds of companies that offer affiliate opportunities. In addition to Amazon, I belong to ShopHer Media, Brand Cycle, ShareASale, LinkShare, and SkimLinks.

Another popular affiliate program is **Rakuten** (formerly "Ebates"). Rakuten is a shopping portal site that pays users a percentage back on their purchases. Shoppers simply create a free Rakuten account and then search the site for the retailer they want to buy from. They click through to the store's site, and Rakuten tracks their spending. Every three months, Rakuten automatically mails out rebate checks.

While I utilize Rakuten for my own shopping rebates, I also use their affiliate program to make money. When you sign up for Rakuten, you are given your own affiliate link to share on social media, including on YouTube. When someone signs up for Rakuten using your affiliate link, you earn $25. Any affiliate income you earn is added to your own rebate check and mailed to you every three months. It is a safe, easy and affective program to increase your overall YouTube earnings.

Referral Links: While affiliate programs pay you in cash, referral links reward you in products. As an example, I belong to several monthly subscription box services, which I review on my personal YouTube channel. If the company has a referral link, I link it in my video. If someone signs up for the subscription using my link, I earn rewards. Sometimes it is points toward free products, other times it's free boxes.

Since affiliate programs pay in cash, I generally prefer them over referral links. However, some companies offer both; and it's then up to me to decide which reward is better. In some cases, I use the affiliate link to earn cash; but in others, I use the referral link to earn free products.

Sponsorships: In addition to earning money through AdSense and affiliate links, you can also bring in cash through sponsorships. A sponsorship is when a company pays you to make a video. If a company has a product to promote, they'll send you the item and pay you to film a video about it. Or, if it's a service, they'll pay you to simply talk about their company.

I was recently sponsored by a major cosmetic brand. They sent me a box of their makeup to review, and I filmed a video of me testing it out. On top of giving me the free products, they also paid me a sponsorship fee.

The more subscribers a channel has, the more lucrative sponsorships can be. Many large YouTube channels make more money from sponsorships than they do from AdSense. It takes a while to build up a large enough audience to start attracting sponsors; I being receiving sponsorship offers when my channel hit 5,000 subscribers. But it depends on what kind of content you are producing and how many actual views your videos typically get.

Selling Your Own Products: From tee shirts and coffee mugs to courses and books, YouTube creators frequently sell their own merchandise, also called "merch". My YouTube channel drives traffic to my Kindle books and to my Ebay store. I don't think I would be as successful as I am with my books if it wasn't for YouTube. Sites like TeeSpring and TeePublic make it easy to create merchandise; I have a TeePublic store this is linked in my YouTube videos, and I sell items there every week. If you have a nickname or tag line, considering slapping it on a tee shirt and offering it up for sale to your YouTube viewers to not only help grow your brand but to also bring in extra money.

CHAPTER 5

MARKETING

There are millions of videos on YouTube. If you want viewers to find your videos, you'll need to take advantage of social networking to market them!

If you really want to establish a presence on YouTube and earn money, you are going to have to do everything you can to promote your channel and your videos. YouTube is a social media platform, and you want to use all of the other social media sites to draw traffic to your videos. Fortunately, these sites are free and easy to use.

Setting up your various social networking sites is another reason why it is so important to choose the best YouTube channel name possible right out of the gate. You want to be known under the same name everywhere to establish your brand. I am "Ann Eckhart" on my blog, YouTube, Facebook, Twitter, Instagram, Pinterest, Tumbler, and Google. I use the same logo across all of my sites, too; so that no matter what site someone is using, when they see "Ann Eckhart" and my logo, they know it is me. My second channel may be called "SeeAnnSell", but I still promote it under my "Ann Eckhart" brand.

While I do YouTube for fun, it is also a business for me. Everything I do in regards to my channel is done to promote it as a brand. My videos drive traffic to my blog and my blog drives traffic to my videos; and both the blog and videos drive traffic to my Kindle books. My blog and my videos both earn AdSense money; so, having them essentially working together increases my ad revenue. My social networking accounts draw traffic to both my blog and YouTube, again resulting in more AdSense dollars. When I added in the YouTube channel to my AdSense account, my earnings doubled from what I had been earning on my blog alone. And all of my sites work to help bring in sponsorships.

Start A Blog: The vast majority of successful YouTubers have coordinating blogs or websites. Most of them actually started off with a blog and then expanded to YouTube. What is great about a blog is that it is an additional way to earn AdSense dollars. When you have both a blog and a YouTube channel that are monetized, you have two sources of AdSense income.

My AdSense earnings doubled when I added my YouTube channel to my account from what I had been earning on my blog alone. And these days, my YouTube AdSense income leaves my blog earnings in the dust.

I personally have my blog set up through BlueHost (bluehost.com) and I use WordPress software. This is a different set up than just starting a free blog on a site such as Blogger (blogger.com) or WordPress (wordpress.org). Since I am using a hosting company, I actually OWN my site. I pay BlueHost for all of their hosting features, one of which is the WordPress software. I decided to go the route of actually paying for my site so that it couldn't be taken down. If Blogger or WordPress were to suddenly shut down (not likely to happen, of course; but you never know), I would still have my website.

Having an actual website that incorporates a blogging platform also allows me many more options for customization. I can do a lot more with my BlueHost site than I could if I was going directly through WordPress. BlueHost offers a bunch of free plug-ins for my site, including many for placing AdSense ads. I simply installed one of the free AdSense plug-ins, clicked where I wanted ads to show, and the ads were automatically placed. I now earn AdSense money from those ads. And I can change the ad placements and sizes at any time.

However, you don't necessarily need to use a paid website to promote your YouTube channel. If you are just starting out, using a free site such as Google or WordPress may be just fine. Here are some of the key differences to help you decide:

Before I started my current blog, I had dabbled in blogging a few different times on Blogger, which is Google's blog platform. I actually had a blog dedicated solely to my Ebay business. However, when I started AnnEckhart.com, I closed the former blog and moved all content to my new website.

The difference between that old Ebay blog and my current AnnEckhart.com blog is that *my Ebay blog was just a blog*, whereas *my AnnEckhart.com blog is technically a website* that hosts my blog. So now I have a blog ON a website.

Confused? Don't worry, I was, and still am sometimes! Even today, I struggle with whether to call AnnEckhart.com a blog or a website. In the beginning, I called it a website, but these days I call it a blog, even though it is actually a website, mainly because the term "blog" is more popular in the social media world. Oy!

To put it simply, a blog that is on a free site such as Blogger or WordPress is just a blog. However, a website is an actual website that you own that utilizes blogging software. AnnEckhart.com is my website, and on my website, I use WordPress blogging software.

When you have a blog on a free site, it is actually not yours but instead belongs to the company behind the site you are using. It could be shut down at any time, and you would then lose all of your content. And while Blogger and WordPress have been around for years and show no signs of going anywhere, the risk is still there that you could eventually lose all of your content.

When I had my Ebay blog on Blogger, I didn't put anything important on it; I just posted about new listings and had the links to my social networking sites. I rarely even promoted the blog; I just maintained it so that if anyone happened to stumble across it, they would hopefully click through to my Ebay store.

However, my AnnEckhart.com blog is actually a business for me as I earn income through affiliate advertising. I also load it with a lot of original content. If it were on a free blogging site, all of that information could be lost in a moment's notice. However, as long as I keep paying my website maintenance fees, my content is safe.

So, if you are just looking for another way to drive traffic to your YouTube channel, stick with creating a simple free blog that has links to your channel and your other social networking sites. Update it whenever you upload a new video and make sure all links are active.

Both Blogger and WordPress offer free blogging platforms. Note, however, that Blogger is owned by Google; therefore, you can link your blog to your AdSense account and earn advertising revenue on BOTH your blog and YouTube channel.

However, if you do decide to go with a paid website, do your research as there are a lot out there to choose from. I went with a large company (bluehost.com) because I wanted my blog to be the centerpiece of my brand and because I wanted to utilize several forms of affiliate advertising on it.

There are a lot of low-cost website options out there. For instance, you can not only register for website URL's on GoDaddy (godaddy.com), but they also offer website hosting along with easy-to-create websites and blogs.

For me, AnnEckhart.com is an actual business, a company that I earn an income from. I share my YouTube videos on my blog whenever I upload a new one, but I also post a lot of other content on my blog such as how to save money shopping and how to make money online. Not to mention the fact that I use my blog to promote my books. For me, my blog encompasses everything I do, not just YouTube.

So, which should you choose? A free blog or a website? Or no site at all? That is a decision only you can make. Having a blog or website for your YouTube channel is NOT a requirement. In fact, it may actually be more work than is worth it for you. And as I talk about in the next chapter, you may find that a Facebook page can just as easily act as your "website".

However, if you do decide to set up a blog or website, it doesn't have to be complicated. Think of it as the "home" page for your brand where you provide the links to your videos as well as to all of your social networking sites (Facebook, Twitter, Pinterest, etc., all of which I'll discuss further in upcoming chapters).

One major benefit of having a blog is that you can run giveaways there. YouTube no longer allows you to host giveaways on your channel or videos. You are not allowed to tie in giveaway requirements to your videos, meaning you can't instruct people to enter a giveaway by subscribing to your channel, giving a video a "thumbs up", or leaving a comment. You can *announce* giveaways in your videos, but you have to direct people somewhere else to enter.

Hence, a blog comes in handy for hosting giveaways as people can enter on the blog. I host weekly giveaways on my blog; I write up a post detailing the giveaway prize, and people enter by leaving comments on the post. I then randomly draw the winner from all of the entries. Because people have to submit their email addresses in order to enter the giveaways, I just email the winner to obtain their mailing address in order to send them their prize.

It's important to note that Facebook has the same policy as YouTube regarding giveaways in that you cannot run them on their site. If you plan to do giveaways, you'll need to have a site other than YouTube or Facebook to host them. You can, however, run the giveaways on Twitter or Instagram (which I'll discuss later on in this book).

Note that in addition to posting updates on your blog, you'll also need to maintain it. If you allow visitors to leave comments on your posts, you'll want to make sure to respond to them. You also want to maintain all links to ensure they are active and up-to-date so that people don't click through and get an error.

As I mentioned in the introduction to this book, if you do start a blog, you'll want to name it the same as your YouTube channel in order to solidify your brand. And you also may want to invest a few dollars in purchasing a dedicated URL.

Facebook If you want to "brand" yourself and your YouTube channel, you'll definitely want to set up a Facebook page. Facebook offers more ways to connect with your audience than Twitter, Pinterest, Instagram, Tumblr, and Google + combined. And if you don't want the hassle of maintaining a blog, a Facebook page can act as your "website".

YouTube makes it easy to share your videos to Facebook as there is a Facebook "share" button located under all videos. Simply click on the Facebook icon, link your YouTube and Facebook accounts together, and you can then share your YouTube videos on your personal and/or business page.

Note that while you may have a personal Facebook account, you will want to set up a Facebook PAGE for your YouTube channel. A Facebook business page is different than a personal Facebook page, although you first need to have a personal Facebook account and page to then set up a business page.

A business page is one people "like", while a personal page is one where people "friend" you. A personal Facebook page has a limit on the number of "friends" you can have, but you can have limitless "likes" on your business page. Having a business page also allows you to separate your personal and public life.

As your YouTube channel grows, you will likely find that viewers want to "friend" you on your personal Facebook page. Even if you aren't promoting your personal page, it will still be easy for most people to find. Unless it is a subscriber you have gotten to know very well, I strongly encourage you NOT to add subscribers as friends on Facebook. You want to maintain privacy with a division between your personal and public/business life. While a lot of my friends and family do "like" my Facebook business page, not all do.

I use my Facebook business page to promote my blog posts and videos; and I save my personal information for my personal Facebook account. While it is hard to turn down friend requests from well-meaning people, for safety and security reasons, I only accept Facebook "friend" requests from my actual friends and family. Blog readers and YouTube subscribers need to "like" my Facebook business page in order to connect with me.

I have set up my personal Facebook page with the tightest security settings to protect myself, and I have turned off the private messaging settings on my business page so that people can't send me messages. When I allowed people to message me, I found myself inundated with long messages from people wanting advice on Ebay, help with couponing, or just someone to chat with. While the vast majority of these messages were harmless, it was taking a lot of my time and energy to deal with all of the questions.

Again, just as it is hard to deny friend requests, it can be hard to ignore messages. However, that is when I remind myself that I am not just doing this for fun but also for profit. I am growing my brand for the long term, and I need to treat it as a business. I also need to protect myself and my family by guarding my personal information as much as possible.

A page needs "likes" in order to grow. While it can take a while to build up the number of "likes" on a business page, I still believe it is important to set one up separate from your personal account. I have seen many people start out using their personal Facebook account for their online content, only to eventually reach the maximum number of "friends" allowed. They then had to scramble to create a business page and encourage everyone to "like" it. Facebook users are more accustomed to "friending" people than "liking" pages, so it does take longer to build a business page than a friend list.

To set up a Facebook business page, simply visit facebook.com/about/pages. You'll need to log into your personal Facebook account first, and then the system will walk you through the steps needed to create your business page. It is FREE and easy to set up.

The first decision you'll need to make is to **name your page**. My Facebook business page is *Ann Eckhart*, which is the same name as my blog and YouTube channel; you'll want your page name to match your YouTube channel name, too.

As you go forward with creating more social media accounts, you'll want your name to be the same across all of them. Remember, the goal is to BRAND yourself so that people will recognize you across all forms of social media. So now is the time to make sure you are happy with your channel name!

There are all kinds of things you can personalize on your Facebook page. You definitely need to add a profile picture and a banner. I have my logo as my profile picture; and I had a custom banner made on **Fiverr** (fiverr.com). Whatever photos or graphics you choose, remember that this is your BUSINESS page, so keep it professional.

You'll also want to fill out the extensive **About** section in order to provide people with information about your YouTube channel. However, since this is your BUSINESS page and separate from your personal page, you'll want to be careful with how much information you provide. While you may share your cell phone number on your personal page, unless you have a brick-and-mortar location that you actually want people to call, you'll want to leave that section blank on your business page.

You'll first need to choose the **Category** for your page; as a YouTube creator, there are several you can choose from such as "Public Figure", "Entertainer", or "Personal Blog or Website" (I prefer the latter; don't dub yourself as a celebrity until you've reached a million subscribers!). You'll need to select a sub-category, too. And don't worry about being locked into your selections; you can easily change them at any time.

In addition to your **Name** (the name of your page, i.e. your YouTube channel name), you can edit your Facebook URL so that it ends in that name.

The **About** section has fields for both a **Short Description** and a **Long Description**. I have my tagline in the Short section and a much more detailed account of what I do in the Long section.

Since you provided information about you and your business in the Short and Long Description sections, use the **General Information** field to share the links to your other social media sites. You'll want to **put the address to your YouTube channel in the main Website field** (remember, your main goal is to drive traffic to your YouTube videos); but add any other links you may have (blog/website, Twitter, Pinterest, Instagram, etc.) to the General Information section so that users can easily connect with you on all of your social media platforms.

Finally, at the top of the page, click on **Settings** to determine how users can interact with you. I have very strict privacy settings for my page. I don't allow people to message me or post on my wall. When I had these two features turned off, I was inundated with messages and posts. However, if getting messages from people is okay with you, then by all means leave those options open. You can always change them later on.

Once you have your page set up, it's time to start building your audience by getting people to "Like" your page. You'll be able to invite the friends and family on your personal page to "Like" your new business page. And of course, you can promote your Facebook page with a YouTube video!

Make sure to provide ACTIVE links under your videos by providing the full URL (i.e. with the "http://" and not just "www"). Putting the full URL will make the links "live" or "active", which means users will be able to click on the links and will then be directly taken to the pages you've linked.

Once you have a Facebook page, as well as other social media accounts, you'll want to make sure to provide links to all of your pages in the information section of your YouTube channel home page as well as under each video. Note that you need to enter in the full URL address of your sites including the "http://" as only the http links will be active, allowing viewers to directly click through to the sites. I have my full description bar write up and links in a Word document that I simply copy and paste into the description box of every video I upload.

As I mentioned earlier, I use my blog and all of my social networking accounts together. When I upload a new YouTube video, I post the link to Facebook. Unfortunately, Facebook has made it more and more difficult for people to see posts, hiding posts from business pages as they want those of us with pages to pay for the posts to be seen.

You've likely noticed the "Boost" buttons under posts that encourage you to pay for your updates to be directly shown to your followers. And while it can be tempting to spend $5 or more to ensure your posts are seen, resist the urge to boost everything you put on Facebook as the results are not worth the cost. Instead perhaps spend $5 every other week or so to boost one post to see if it has an effect on your page "likes" and/or on your YouTube subscriber growth.

Because Facebook is selective about what posts they will show your followers, it's important to do more than just post links to your Facebook page in order to engage your audience. Facebook prefers original posts and photos over links that you simply copy and paste to your page. I try to post a regular status update at least once a day, which is more likely to be shown to my followers than a post with a link that I share directly from my blog. I also occasionally share photos on my Facebook page; like status updates, photos tend to show up to more people than just links to my blog.

Another way to engage your Facebook page users is to post "teasers" for upcoming videos. Post a photo of yourself as you are prepping to film, or a picture of something you are getting ready to share, with the message that a new video will be coming the next day. This will get people excited for your newest video to be released.

You want to encourage people to "like" and "comment" on your Facebook posts in the hopes their activity will show up on their friends' feeds, which will help more people come to your page. You have likely seen this happen on your Facebook feed where it will show you that a friend liked a post or a page. The convenient "like" thumbs up icon will be there, making it easy for you, too, to "like" the page.

It is always my hope that when someone "likes" one of my posts that their friends will see it, check out my page, and then "like" it, too. As I mentioned earlier, Facebook shows status updates and photos more than links; so, I get more "likes" and comments on my status updates and photos than I do when I simply share links to my blog posts or videos.

As I mentioned earlier, you may decide that a Facebook page can act as your blog or website rather than setting up a separate site. Many YouTube creators do not have a blog or website, rather using Facebook as their homepage. So, unless you have the time to devote to maintaining a separate website, consider just using Facebook along with other social networking to promote your Ebay business. I recommend you do Facebook FIRST as you can always add a blog/website later on.

Twitter: If you don't already have a Twitter account, you can create one for FREE at Twitter.com. If you do have an account that you are active on, consider creating a new one just for your YouTube channel. As with Facebook, you want to keep your personal and business lives separate on Twitter. Make sure your Twitter handle is the same as your YouTube channel. Remember, part of branding is being known as ONE name across ALL social media platforms.

Like Facebook, Twitter provides a free and easy way to connect with viewers and drive traffic to your videos. YouTube makes sharing your videos to Twitter super easy as there is a Twitter share button under all videos. Simply click on the Twitter icon and link your YouTube account to your Twitter account to share the title of your video as well as the direct link.

Twitter allows users to share posts of 140 characters or less. While the title of your video and the link will automatically be put into the Twitter field, you can increase your exposure by adding hashtags. Hashtags are simply keywords that follow a pound (#) sign. For instance, when I do a video about an extreme couponing Target haul, I will add in hashtags such as #Target, #ExtremeCouponing, #ExtremeCouponer, #couponing, #coupons, #haul, and #shopping. Savvy Twitter users search for Tweets using hashtags, so adding them to your Twitter posts is another way to drive traffic to your videos.

I set aside some time every evening to connect with other Twitter users since I can do this on my iPhone while relaxing in front of the TV. I follow other bloggers and YouTube creators, retweet posts I like, reply to posts, and post a Tweet or two of my own. Twitter works best when you actively engage with other users, so it's important to spend some time each day networking on Twitter so that you can grow your followers.

Some Twitter users follow everyone who follows them; and this can certainly be a way to build up your followers. You can also "network" with other folks on Twitter by replying to, retweeting, or favoring tweets. As I mentioned when setting up your Facebook page, you can add all of your social media links, including your Twitter URL, in the "About" section; so hopefully some of your Facebook fans will follow you to Twitter. To encourage this, about once a week post your

Twitter link directly to your Facebook page to make it easy for people to click through and "follow" you.

Add your Twitter URL to the list of other links you share on your YouTube channel, both in your channel information section as well as under each video. Remember to add the http:// to your link to make it active so that users can directly click through to your Twitter account.

The "edit profile" feature located on your Twitter homepage allows you to customize the look and information people will see when they click on your profile. Add a nice, clear photo of yourself (or your logo, if you have one); and add a header image. Write up a brief but fun description of yourself. Put the link to your YouTube channel in the website field so that people can click through to your videos. And finally, click on "theme colors" to customize your profile page even further.

Personalizing your Twitter profile and then engaging with other users every day will result in more and more people finding your YouTube videos and subscribing to your channel!

Pinterest: Pinterest is often overlooked when it comes to promoting YouTube videos; but, as with Facebook and Twitter, it's another free and easy way to drive traffic to your channel and increase your video views. And increased views mean more AdSense dollars!

You can create a FREE Pinterest page at pinterest.com.

Pinterest allows you to create "boards" where you "pin" content. You can "pin" content that others have posted, and you can also share your own "pins". Pinterest started out as a way for people, mainly women, to "pin" craft ideas and recipes to virtual boards. However, Pinterest is quickly becoming a tool for businesses to get the word out about their products and to develop brand loyalty. And as you grow your YouTube brand, you'll want to make Pinterest a part of your marketing strategy!

I have a board on Pinterest named "YouTube Videos". As with Facebook and Twitter, YouTube provides a "share" icon for Pinterest underneath all videos. After I upload a video to YouTube, I simply click on the Pinterest icon and "pin" it to my "YouTube Videos" board. The video then appears on the feed of those who follow me on Pinterest. They can click through to my video directly from my pin. And if they "repin" the post, then their followers will also see it. I have noticed a dramatic increase to my blog and YouTube traffic since I started pinning my blog posts and videos to Pinterest.

Just as you should be doing with your Facebook and Twitter links, be sure to link your Pinterest page in your YouTube channel profile as well as in the description bar underneath all of your videos. And put the link in the General Information section of your Facebook page. Be sure to periodically share your Pinterest link on both Facebook and Twitter in order to attract new followers.

You may be noticing by now that a big part of social networking is to have all of your sites working together. Include all of your social media links on your blog/website and on Facebook. Post your Twitter and

Pinterest links to Facebook; share your Facebook and Pinterest links on Twitter. The more you can get your YouTube channel link out there, the easier it will be for people to find your videos and for your channel to grow!

Instagram: Instagram offers another free, easy and fun way to interact with your YouTube subscribers and to gain more viewers. Instagram allows you to share photos, as well as to "like" and comment on photos shared by others. While you can put a full-length YouTube video onto Pinterest, you can share content and put in links to your channel, both with your photos and in your profile.

To create a FREE Instagram account, simply visit Instagram.com. Again, make sure your Instagram name is the same as your YouTube channel and all other social media sites.

The best use of Instagram that I have found is to connect with subscribers on a more personal level. While I mainly talk about couponing, shopping and Ebay information in my YouTube videos, I share personal photos of my dogs and family on Instagram. I will also share photos of fun activities such as dinner out or local events. And I also post pictures of my shopping hauls. Whatever the photo content, however, the main goal is to further connect with followers who are interested in the content I am providing, whether it is on my blog or on my YouTube channel.

Hashtags are a big part of getting your content on Instagram found. I like to include three to five hashtags with every photo I share. When I post a photo related to a Dollar Tree haul video, for instance, I use hashtags such as #haul, #dollartree, #dollartreehaul, #shopping, and/or #youtubecreator. The goal of these hashtags is that many people will search for them and find me. Even if they don't end up following me on Instagram, they still may check out my profile and click through to my blog.

Instagram allows you to include one website link in your profile; but you can use a site called Linktree (linktr.ee) to put multiple links in your profile. Linktree allows you to create a menu of all of your links; there is then one link in your profile that takes viewers to your Linktree page. Linktree is free and easy to use; and you can edit your links anytime you'd like. In my Linktree menu, I have my blog, YouTube channel, Facebook page, Twitter account, and TeePublic site listed.

When promoting my YouTube channel via Instagram, I post a thumbnail from my most recent video and encourage followers to head over to my channel to watch it. Since the link to my YouTube channel is in my Linktree menu, which is linked in my bio, I usually write: "New video now live on my YouTube channel; direct link in my profile @ann_eckhart. The "@" link will take users to my profile page where the active link to my Linktree menu, and therefore my YouTube channel, will be. Then the user simply clicks on my YouTube channel URL, taking then straight to my videos.

Once you reach 10,000 Instagram followers, you can add "swipe up" links into your Instagram stories. After I share about a new video on my main Instagram feed, I also post about it in my Instagram stories with a direct link to the video so that people can "swipe up" to watch it.

As with Twitter and Pinterest, it's a good idea to actively network with others on Instagram by following them back, "liking" their pictures, and leaving comments. I like to spend about 10 minutes a day scrolling through my Instagram feed to check out what others are posting and to engage with my favorite posts.

Note, also, that Instagram is an app. While you can see your Instagram feed, edit your profile, and add followers on a computer, you can only add your own posts using the app on your smart phone or tablet.

Tumblr: Tumblr (tumblr.com) is a micro-blogging and social networking site that allows you to share content in a somewhat similar way to Pinterest in that you create original posts or share the posts of others. There are some people, mostly celebrities and brands, who use Tumblr as their blog with it acting as the main landing page for their business.

There are a lot of bloggers and brands on Tumblr, giving it a sort-of magazine feel. It's free and easy to create an account; and most blog platforms as well as YouTube provide easy "share" buttons that allow to you quickly post your content to your Tumblr page.

You can get as fancy as you want with Tumblr, changing up the theme and design. And you can authorize Google, Twitter, Facebook, and

Instagram to automatically connect with your Tumblr account to share content and to find your friends who are on the site.

So how can Tumblr work to increase your video views? I use Tumblr the same way I use Google+, which is as a free and easy "extra" in my social media arsenal. I don't spend much time on Tumblr other than to share my blog posts, YouTube videos, and Instagram photos. I have my settings set so that these posts are all automatically shared, meaning I don't have to manually do it. I haven't spent much time seeking out followers or following others on the site; but I do get periodic notification that another Tumblr user has started following me.

Depending on what types of videos you make, you may want to put more effort into Tumblr than I do. My YouTube videos are a blend of my See Ann Save content: shopping, hauls, vlogs, and Ebay. Since Tumblr posts tend to lean more towards fashion and entertainment, my content doesn't exactly appeal to the site's target audience. But again, since it's free and easy, I still post my links there.

What I recommend is that you sign up for a Tumblr account and then see if other people who make videos similar to yours are also on the site. Also, look at the brands and entertainers you like to see if you have content that aligns with theirs. The Tumblr audience tends to skew younger, so depending on your age, you may find yourself really liking it or feeling a bit bewildered (I'm the latter!).

Network with Fellow Youtubers: There is a fine line between networking with other YouTube creators in order to grow your channel and outright using them to help you. One of the most painful things I see new YouTubers do is BEGGING people to subscribe to their channel. They stalk the successful YouTube channels and leave comments asking the viewers of someone else's channel to sub their channel, too. Or worse, they send out private messages to the subscribers of other channels begging them to subscribe.

If you are creating quality content, there is no reason to beg for subscribers. In fact, it is so tacky and frowned upon nowadays that you will likely turn off potential viewers. However, there are ways that you can network with other YouTube creators that is beneficial for both you and them.

First of all, you want to SUPPORT other channels. Subscribe to the channels you like, give their videos a thumbs up, leave nice comments, and share their videos via your social networks (I like to share my favorite videos to both Twitter and Pinterest using the "share" buttons located under each video). Showing your support to other channels not only helps out your favorite YouTube creators, but it will likely get you noticed by their subscribers, drawing people to your channel.

If you do develop a friendly "relationship" with another YouTuber (they are replying to your comments or noticing your Tweets), THEN it is okay to casually mention that you also make videos.

If you find another YouTube creator with the same number of subscribers as you have and who is creating similar content, you may want to suggest doing a collaboration video with them. Lots of

YouTubers do "collabs" where they partner with another channel to create videos with a similar theme. Ideas include sending each other boxes of goodies to open on camera, answering "tag" questions, or participating in group challenges. If you live in the same area, you can actually film videos together, each posting a video to your respective channels and then directing viewers to go to the other channel to watch the other video.

Not only do collaboration videos help you to make friends in the YouTube community, everyone benefits by encouraging viewers to check out all of the channels that are participating. People who do collab videos link each other's channels in their video's description bar and the videos are then shared via social media.

One thing you absolutely do NOT want to do is pay for subscribers. There are online companies that, for a price, will get people (usually automated computer "robots") to subscribe to your channel. However, VIEWS are what create AdSense revenue, not subscribers. People who have been paid to subscribe to a channel will not actually watch the videos. Plus, there are sites that track YouTube channel subscribers, views and revenue, so it's obvious when someone has paid for subscribers as there will be a sudden huge spike in their numbers.

Create great content, support the channels you enjoy watching, utilize your social media accounts, and let the viewers and subscribers build naturally! After all, you want people to actually WATCH your videos, not just hit subscribe because they've been paid or guilted into doing so.

CHAPTER 6

BEST PRACTICES

Film quality and marketing aren't enough when it comes to gaining viewers and subscribers. Follow these best practices to ensure your YouTube career is a success!

Begging: As I talked about earlier, one of the most painful things I see new YouTubers do is BEGGING people to subscribe to their channel. They stalk the successful YouTube channels and leave comments asking those viewers to sub their channel, too. Or worse, they send out private messages to the subscribers of other channels begging them to subscribe.

If you are creating quality content, there is no reason to beg for subscribers. In fact, it is so tacky and frowned upon nowadays that you will likely turn off viewers

As I talked about earlier, you also don't want to pay for subscribers. There are online companies that, for a price, will drive people to subscribe to your channel. However, as I said before, VIEWS are what create AdSense revenue, not subscribers. People who have been paid to subscribe to a channel will not actually watch the videos. Plus, there are sites that track YouTube channel subscribers, views and revenue, so it's obvious when someone has paid for subscribers as there will be a sudden huge spike in their numbers.

Produce content you enjoy making, have fun, and the subscribers, views and PROFIT will follow!

Channel Design: When you log into YouTube, you can click on "My Channel" to edit the design of your channel's homepage. You can add a logo, choose a channel trailer, and even include links to your blog and social networking sites. Don't ignore this page as it goes a long way towards building your brand and establishing your YouTube channel.

I usually change my channel trailer weekly so that one of my most current videos appears; you can also create a special "channel introduction" video to have up at all times for new subscribers.

Description Box: When you upload a video to YouTube, you need to create a title and put some information into the description box that is below each video. I will share what is in my description box in the next section of this book. Your description box should give your viewers directions for what you want them to do; and the first two things should be the most important as those are the only things viewers will initially see unless they expand the view to reveal everything written in the box.

Some YouTubers ask views to give their videos a thumbs-up, leave a comment and subscribe as the first things in their description boxes. For me, since I am trying to drive traffic to my books, I list my Amazon Author Page first. Under that I have all of the links to my social networking sites, a bit about me, and my disclaimer. If I am ending my video by directing people to my social networking sites, I tell them that all of my links are listed in the description box below and that they just have to click on the down arrow to bring everything into view.

I keep the verbiage that is in the description box of my videos in a Word document so that I can simply copy/paste the information whenever I upload a new video. Because viewers only see the first three lines of the description bar unless they click to expand it, it's important to put your most important directive there. Make sure any websites you link have the full URL addresses so that they will be "live", i.e. so viewers can click on them and be taken directly to your site.

Encouraging Likes, Comments & Subscriptions: While it may seem logical that people who watch and enjoy your videos will give them a "thumbs up", leave a comment, and subscribe to your channel, the vast majority of viewers will not give you any sort of feedback whatsoever. As I mentioned earlier, many people will find your videos through internet searches or shares on Google+. Most don't even have a YouTube account, so they can't respond to your videos in any way.

For viewers who do have a YouTube account, however, you want to encourage interaction as much as possible. YouTube offers those with a YouTube account the ability to "like" (i.e. click on the little "thumbs up" icon) videos; leave a comment under videos; subscribe to channels; add videos to a "favorites" list; and share videos to their social media accounts. Encouraging people to do any of the above helps to promote your videos as the friends and followers of those viewers will see their activity and possibly follow suit.

At the end of most of my videos, I will ask people to leave me any questions or comments they might have. I will also ask that if they liked the video to "give it a thumbs-up". Finally, I suggest that they subscribe for more videos. Some YouTube creators ask for likes and subscribers at the beginning of their videos. What you do is up to you; you can always play around with this to see what feels the most natural.

Monitoring Comments: Having viewers leave comments on your videos is something every YouTuber appreciates…unless those comments are mean. While the vast majority of comments on my videos are positive, every now and again a "hater" comes along and says something rude or nasty. The more views a video gets, the more likely it is that someone will eventually leave a negative comment on it. The large YouTube channels whose videos get millions of views have to deal with an enormous amount of hate, some of it so bad that it has driven successful YouTubers off of the site.

Some YouTubers do not monitor the comments left on their videos, believing that free speech protects those who leave comments. While I am all for free speech, I believe it comes with consequences. And the consequence for someone leaving a negative comment on one of my videos is that I remove the comment and ban the person from my channel so that they can't interact with me on YouTube in any way (either by giving a video a thumbs down, leaving me a comment, or sending me a message). My YouTube channel is my personal space. I wouldn't allow someone to come into my home and treat me poorly, so I am not going to allow them to be mean to me through YouTube.

As I said, however, the vast majority of people who leave comments are kind and supportive. I try my best to reply to anyone who leaves a comment on any of my videos, although I usually only do this for the first day or two after the video goes live. While YouTube used to send a message to you every time a new comment was left on one of your videos, they no longer do this. You do get a notification of activity on your videos whenever you log in (there will be a little red box next to the bell icon at the top of the page with the number of activities – likes, comments, shares, subscriptions – that are new), but it's now a lot harder to find and reply to comments, especially on older videos.

Often people will continue to leave comments on videos months or even years after they were first put up, and responding to those can be nearly impossible. Do the best you can to reply to comments, or at least acknowledge that you are reading all comments in your videos. You want to continually let your audience know that you appreciate all of their "likes" and comments!

Having viewers leave comments on your videos is something every YouTuber appreciates...unless those comments are mean. While the vast majority of comments on my videos are positive, every now and again a "hater" comes along and says something rude or nasty. The more views a video gets, the more likely it is that someone will eventually leave a negative comment on it. The large YouTube channels whose videos get millions of views have to deal with an enormous amount of hate, some of it so bad that it has driven successful YouTubers off of the site.

Some YouTubers do not monitor the comments left on their videos, believing that free speech means people can say whatever they please. While I am all for free speech, I believe it comes with consequences. And the consequence for someone leaving a negative comment on one of my videos is that I remove the comment and ban the person from my channel so that they can't leave comments on my videos or send me messages. My YouTube channel is my personal space. I wouldn't allow someone to come into my home and treat me poorly, so I am not going to allow them to be mean to me through YouTube.

However, even if you don't get rude comments, you will likely get the occasionally "thumbs down". I am currently averaging about five dislikes on all of my videos; I honestly think they are from people who subscribe to my channel just so they can dislike my videos when they go live! While it's never a good feeling to see a dislike, realize that almost every single person who makes YouTube videos gets them; and the more views a video gets, the more dislikes it will have. This is just the nature of YouTube, so try to accept it and move on, focusing on the likes and positive comments you do receive.

As I said, the vast majority of people who leave comments on my videos are kind and supportive. I try my best to reply to anyone who leaves a nice comment on any of my videos, even if it is just a simple "thank you".

When you are in the "Video Manager" screen of your YouTube account, you can click on the "Community" link on the left side of the page to see all of the comments that have been left on all of your videos with the newest comments listed first. This is much easier than going into every video individually to see the comments. You can reply to the comments right in the "Community" screen. And you can also remove comments and spam as well as block users there, too.

Often people will continue to leave comments on videos months or even years after they were first put up. Do the best you can to reply to comments, or at least give comments the "thumbs up". You want to continually let your audience know that you appreciate all of their support!

Privacy: When the internet first became available, people could hide anonymously behind their computers, posting whatever they wanted under screen names without anyone knowing who or where they were. However, social media, and especially YouTube, has changed that. Even if you decide to make videos where you don't appear on screen, you will still be exposing yourself to the world. Therefore, it's important to take the proper safety and security measures.

Keep the exact location of your home to yourself. I only ever say that I live in Iowa; I don't mention the exact city. I don't show the front of my house. I have a P.O. Box set up for mail so that I don't have to give out my home address. I don't announce if I am going on vacation, not only so that people don't know I'm not home but so that they don't know where I will be. Now, I am a small time YouTuber, and these measures may seem extreme. However, it's the level of privacy that I am most comfortable with. I would rather be safe than sorry!

Schedule & Consistency: If you are on YouTube to make money and build your brand, you are going to want to keep a consistent schedule of uploading videos. Some people upload on a certain day of the week while others aim for a set number of videos per week. Since I only create content that I truly enjoy, I only upload videos when I have something I want to share. Sometimes this means I upload several videos in a week, while other times I may only do one.

However, unless something has happened to prevent me from making a video (such as if I have gotten sick), I don't go more than a week without uploading a video. In general, I average about four videos a week. This keeps subscribers happy as they are getting consistent content, and it helps to attract new viewers to my channel as my video selection grows.

Nothing is worse that subscribing to a new YouTuber who promises frequent videos, only to never see them again. If you are going to be successful on YouTube, you HAVE to commit to it. You can't upload a few videos, abandon your channel, and then wonder why you don't have any subscribers and aren't making any money. Find a filming schedule that works for you and stick to it!

YouTube analytics and viewers prefer videos that are around 15 minutes in length. Unless you are a filming a vlog-style video or doing a live question and answer session or hangout, anything longer than 15 minutes is usually too long for most people. However, putting up videos that are too short may not satisfy viewers. And if viewers don't watch, you won't earn any AdSense revenue. I watch channels that put up 10-minute videos and others that produce videos over an hour. Again, sticking to your guns and creating the content that pleases you is the most important thing, regardless of video length.

However, more important than the length of videos is the QUALITY of them. You don't need expensive camera equipment or editing software to produce quality YouTube videos (I film and upload videos on an iPhone), but you do want your videos to be clear, steady, and well lit. Speak up so viewers can hear you.

Watch your video back before you upload it and make it live to ensure it looks nice. I'd rather reshoot a video or skip it altogether than upload one that is poor quality. When I upload my videos, I have them set to "Private" so that I can review them on YouTube before I make them public. And as my filming has gotten better over the years, I've actually deleted old videos that weren't up to my standards and reshot others.

URL: I own the URL addresses for See Ann Save in just about every configuration possible (.com, .net, see-ann-save), as well as several other website address for my name. Since I have a blog, YouTube channel, and books, it's an important part of my "branding" strategy that I have control over my web presence.

You can easily and relatively inexpensively get a personalized URL from a site such as GoDaddy.com. You can then point that URL directly to your YouTube channel. Or if you have a blog like I do, you can point your URL there. I direct people to my blog at SeeAnnSave.com where they can then find the links for all of my social networking sites, including YouTube.

Video Length: YouTube analytics and viewers prefer videos that are around 10 minutes in length. I film a lot of different types of videos for my channel, including vlogs, couponing tutorials, shopping hauls, and information about Ebay. My videos average around 15 minutes; vlogs are longer while unboxings and reviews tend to be shorter. I try not to worry so much about the length of the video; rather, it's important to focus on the quality of content.

Views vs. Subscribers: Most people start off on YouTube focused solely on gaining subscribers. And while the number of subscribers you have is important in the overall growth of your channel and your brand, more important is the number of views your videos get.

I have seen people worried so much about gaining subscribers that they have actually PAID people to subscribe to their channels. However, just because someone subscribes to your channel doesn't mean they will actually watch your videos. You only earn AdSense revenue from people WATCHING your videos, so paying for subscribers is a huge waste of time and money.

Only when someone watches your monetized videos and sees or clicks on the ads that are there will you earn any Google AdSense revenue. In order to attract viewers, you need to produce quality content. Not all subscribers will watch all of your videos, and not all viewers will become subscribers. If you have one of two videos that draw a lot of viewers from internet searches or Google +, you may end up making a lot of AdSense money from people just watching your videos, even if they don't end up subscribing.

If you are like me, however, and you are doing YouTube for both profit AND fun, then you will be consistently uploading new videos. While I have a handful of videos with current views in the tens of thousands, as of this writing the majority of my videos average about 2,000 views each within the first week, some a bit less and some a bit more. Of course, the longer my videos remain on YouTube, the more views they will get. Your videos will continue to earn AdSense money as long as people continue to watch them!

I focus on creating quality content that I am personally interested in with the hopes that the viewers will respond. While my videos work in conjunction with my blog to bring in AdSense revenue, I never make a video thinking that it is going to make me money. I make videos that I enjoy filming and that I hope others will benefit from. Sometimes my favorite videos are the least viewed. However, I just continue making the videos I want to make, and eventually like-minded people find them.

Making videos is a time-consuming process, so if I am not having fun, I'm not going to do it. Viewers are smart and will see right through attempt to film videos that are strictly done for views. Be yourself, have fun, and the views and subscribers will come!

Monetizing Your Videos: Just because your channel has been approved for monetization doesn't mean that you will automatically start earning AdSense income. You have to MANUALLY turn the AdSense on in each of your videos. This is easy to do in the YouTube Studio section of your account. Simply go into the "Video Details" section of your latest video and click on the "Monetization" tab on the left. On the "Video Monetization" page, select "On" from the "Monetization" drop-down menu. Then click on every box under "Type of Ads". If your video is over 10 minutes long, you'll be able to run ads during the video. These "mid-break ad rolls" are essential for increasing your earnings. Once I started enabling ads to run during my videos, not just before and after, my AdSense immediately doubles.

CHAPTER 7

DAY IN THE LIFE

Being a YouTuber involves more than just uploading videos. Here is an example of everything I have to do to film, edit, upload, and release a YouTube video!

A couple of years ago, I went to Walgreens every Sunday to shop the deals using coupons with my goal being to demonstrate to my blog readers and YouTube subscribers how to save money at the drugstore chain. After shopping, I would write up my haul for my blog AND film a coordinating YouTube video. While it would seem that reporting on a simple shopping trip would be easy, the process of creating the content actually took a few hours. Here is I went through to film a typical shopping trip:

Before going to Walgreens, I first had to plan my trip. I did this part off-camera, as it's not very exciting to watch me scour the coupon matching websites and clip coupons. I started working on my shopping list on Thursday when the first reports of the upcoming ad came out. I then revised my plan over the next few days, gathering the coupons I needed and writing my shopping plan down.

On Sunday morning, I pulled the Walgreens weekly ad and coupon inserts from the Sunday paper. I cut out more coupons from the inserts, as well as some coupons from the Walgreens ad. I also cut out the deals I wanted to get from the Walgreens ad and pasted them onto a piece of paper. That way I had all of the offers I was looking for on one page rather than having to leaf through the entire ad while in the store.

Once I had my list, my page of deals, my coupons, and my Walgreens Balance Rewards Card, I headed out to Walgreens. I didn't film inside of the store on this trip, although sometimes I do record when I am actually shopping. I spent about 20 minutes in the store filling up my cart and then checking out. On this day, the cash register froze up and there were a couple of issues with my coupons, so check out took a bit longer than usual.

When I was finally done checking out, I headed back home. I took my bags into my office and unpacked my purchases. I have a table set up in my office for taking pictures and filming hauls, so I set up everything so that I could get a nice picture. Once the photo of the entire haul was taken, edited, and saved to my computer, I started working on my blog post. I typed up everything I bought, including links to the coupons I used and the rewards I earned. I added in the photo, and I then published the blog. I then posted the link to the blog post to Facebook, Twitter, and Pinterest. I also posted the photo of the haul to Instagram.

After my blog post went live, I went back to my table and started filming my YouTube video. I turned on all of my lights and made sure my iPhone was turned horizontally to film. On this day, we were having a thunderstorm and both of my dogs were barking because of the noise. It took me five tries before I was able to record the full video!

After going through all of the deals I got, I ended the video by asking viewers to leave me any comments or questions they may have had. I also asked that they give the video a "thumbs up" if they liked it; and I encouraged them to subscribe to my channel for more couponing videos.

Note that for this video, I held the camera and showed the haul, rather than appearing myself on camera and holding up products. I film both ways for my channel depending on the content and how I am feeling. For videos where I appear on screen, I usually skip the tripod and just prop my iPhone up on some books. Nothing too fancy for my filming set ups!

Once I was happy with the footage of my Walgreens haul, I sat down to start work on the uploading process. First, I opened up the iMovie app on my iPhone and moved the still photo I had taken for my blog into the first position on the project. Sometimes I like to make a photo the first shot in iMovie when I do hauls as it gives a nice opening to the video. Since I had shot the entire haul in one video clip, I only had to move the one block of film into iMovie behind the photo. If I was doing a vlog, I would have had numerous clips to put together in iMovie; however, when filming hauls and reviews, I am usually able to film everything in one shot.

After both clips were in iMovie, I saved the project to my camera roll in HD 720p, which is high-definition. I clicked on the YouTube icon and choose to upload the clip in HD 720p. While I had saved the clip in HD 720p, I still needed to select the high-definition option to upload it that way to YouTube. Since you have to upload HD via Wi-Fi, if anything disrupts your connection during the uploading process, the upload will fail and you have to restart the whole process.

Another issue I have with my iPhone is that I have to make sure my phone stays "awake" during the uploading process. If my settings kick in and my phone turns off, then the uploading process is stopped and I have to restart it all over again. So, it's important that I remember to turn sleep mode OFF before I start uploading. Videos under 10 minutes usually upload in under a minute, but the upload time increases with longer videos.

In order to upload from my phone, I have to name the video and put something in the description box. When uploading, I just choose one word for each field rather than writing out the full descriptions, which I can do from my computer when the video is uploaded.

Finally, I ALWAYS make sure to set the video to "Private" when I am uploading as I will need to do some more editing before it goes live. Choosing "Private" means only you will be able to see the video once you are logged into your YouTube account. If you have "Public" selected, the video will be live once the upload is complete. After you've edited it, you can make it "Public", which means it will be live for your subscribers and anyone else with YouTube access to see.

On this day, the uploading process went smoothly. Once my video was successfully uploaded, I went onto YouTube from my laptop. I have both an iPhone and a Kindle HDX, but I can only edit my videos on YouTube from my laptop.

In my YouTube video manager page, I wrote out a keyword-loaded title and filled in the description field with all of my blog and social networking links. As I showed you earlier in this book, I copied my description box information from a Word document and pasted it into the description field under the video.

If I have an accompanying blog post or additional referral links (such as for a subscription box I am reviewing), I will include those links in the description field, too. On this day, I also included the link to the blog post where I detailed my Walgreens trip, which provided the direct links to the coupons I used.

After filling out the description area, I started adding "tags" to the tag field. Tags are keywords that people use to search YouTube with. I filled up the tag area with all of the keywords that related to that days Walgreens haul. I typed in lots of key words and phrases, separating them all by commas: Walgreens, couponing, coupons, extreme couponer, extreme couponing, Register Rewards, Balance Rewards, couponing at Walgreens, Walgreens haul, drugstore shopping, haul, Almay, Burt's Bees, Reese's, Ziploc, Ban, Crest, Tresemme.

In 2019, YouTube added the option to include three hashtags to the description box that appear at the top of your video. So, for this video I would have put the hashtags #walgreens #coupons #extremecouponing at the very bottom of the description box field; they would then show up at the top of the video. The purpose of this is that your video tags will link to other videos with the same tags. Let's say another YouTuber also has the hashtag #walgreens in their video. If a viewer clicks on that tag, it will show other videos with the same tags. It's just another way to potentially draw new viewers to your channels.

Once all of the fields were filled out but while the video was still set to private, I watched it back to catch any mistakes. I soon realized that when referring to Balance Rewards POINTS that I was saying DOLLARS. When I should have said that I earned "5,000 Balance Rewards points on the Burt's Bees product", I instead stated that I earned "5,000 DOLLARS". Oops! However, instead of re-filming the entire video and going through the uploading process again, I instead clicked on the "Annotations" tab at the top of the screen and added a "speech bubble" to the video explaining the mistake. I was able to adjust the length of how long I wanted to "bubble" to appear, and I even make it pink with white text to make it clearer for the viewers.

One last step before making the video live was to monetize it. In the video editing screen is a monetization tab on the left-hand side of the screen. I clicked on that tab, checked the box for monetization, and then hit save. Sometimes videos are monetized immediately, while other times they go into for review and take a while to be approved. This is why I film and upload videos a few days in advance; in case my video goes into the review process, I have enough time to request a manual review to get it monetized.

After the video was monetized and I was satisfied with the title, description box, and tags, I scheduled the video to go live on the date and at the time I upload videos. I like to make videos go live on the same days and at the same times so that subscribers know when to expect uploads from me. YouTube also favors videos that upload on a consistent schedule.

Once my video was live, I clicked on the heading so that it took me to the live screen (i.e. out of the video manager page). I could now see what my video looked like to the public, whether they were a subscriber or just someone who found it on their own. Visible to only me under the video were the editing options, so I could quickly go back to the video manager section by clicking on any of those options. However, viewers don't see those links on their feed, just the video and description field.

Under all YouTube videos are "Share" options for Facebook, Twitter, Tumbler, Pinterest, and more. I share my videos to Facebook, Twitter, and Pinterest. On Facebook and Twitter, I add in hashtags, which are keywords behind a # sign. On this day, I choose hashtags such as #Walgreens, #ExtremeCouponer and #drugstorehaul, depending how much space was available on each site.

Clicking on the share links usually places the title and the video link to the social networking site you choose. However, on Tumbler, I have to automatically write in the title. I also have to choose which board to pin my video to on Pinterest; I have a YouTube Video board set up, so I select that option.

Also, under "Share" is an "Embedded" choice. Embedded gives me the HTML code so that I can place the video over on my blog. For this particular video, I copied the HTML code, went back to my blog, opened up the editing window on the blog post, and placed the code in my post. I then resaved the blog post so that my video now appeared along with the original content.

I also have a "Videos" page set up on my blog, the link for which appears in the bar at the top of my site. On this page, I talk a bit about my YouTube channel and direct people there to see all of my videos. I also have several of my most recent videos on the page for people to watch, so on this day I added the embedded code for the video to the page, taking off the video that had been up the longest so that only five appeared. I only have five videos so that the files don't slow down my site and so that only the most recent content is on the page.

Over the next day or so, I replied to the comments that people left on the video. YouTube used to send you a message anytime someone left a comment on your videos, but they have stopped doing that; therefore, it's important to be proactive in monitoring comments.

So, between first preparing for my shopping trip and finally replying to comments, I probably spent three hours in total on a Walgreens haul blog post and YouTube video. That is a lot of time and effort for videos that averaged under 15 minutes each!

I'm currently uploading vlogs every single day on my SeeAnnSell YouTube channel. I also film sit-down videos for my Ann Eckhart channel. The process for all of my videos is the same as with the couponing video I referenced above:

- Using my iPhone and holding it horizontally, I film various clips during the day
- I put all of the clips together in iMovie,
- I save the finished video to my camera roll at 750HD

- If the video is over 10 minutes, I made sure to turn the sleep mode off on my phone so as my camera won't switch off during the uploading process

- I open up the YouTube app and click on the little camera icon

- I choose the video from my camera roll

- I type one word into the title and description field and make sure the video is set to private

- I then click upload

- Once the video is uploaded, I switch over to my computer

- I add in my title, fill out the description box, add in any hashtags, monetize the video, and schedule it for the time and date I want it to go live

With all of the work involved, why do I make YouTube videos? Because it is FUN! I love connecting with other resellers through my Ebay videos on my SeeAnnSell YouTube channel; and I also love to share shopping hauls and subscription box videos on my Ann Eckhart channel. However, not only are the videos fun to make, they earn me AdSense. My videos also bring traffic to my Amazon Author Page, where I sell my books. Sometimes viewers buy the merchandise I have for sale in my TeePublic store. And being on YouTube also gives me to opportunity to receive free products as well as sponsorships.

For fun AND profit – that is why I do YouTube!

CONCLUSION

With a camera and computer, anyone can start a YouTube channel. However, it takes commitment and perseverance to make MONEY on YouTube. While there are some people who have gotten rich by making videos, for most people, YouTube offers a bit of extra money. How much you earn is up to you in terms of how much time and effort you are willing to put into producing quality content that viewers respond to.

Putting yourself out there in front of thousands and potentially millions of people is a scary proposition. However, if you approach YouTube for your own personal enjoyment and growth before anything else, you will have a successful channel that also brings you some income!

As the saying goes, do what you love and the money will follow. On YouTube, have FUN, and you will also see the PROFIT add up!

ABOUT THE AUTHOR

Ann Eckhart is a writer, blogger, YouTube creator, social media influencer, and Ebay seller based in Iowa. She has numerous books available on topics including selling on Ebay, saving money, and making money online. For more information, visit her website at AnnEckhart.com.

Made in the USA
Columbia, SC
28 December 2019

85910482R00055